The

Debris Monitor's

Guide

Written by
Colin Keogh

2nd Edition
Copyright 2018

I want to thank the many people that have helped me, trained me and supported me while writing this book. Susan, Kelli, Craig, Tommy, Ron, Cory, Keith, Brent, Jessie, and Lamar; your support, knowledge, and friendship have made this book possible. Each of you helped me learn important lessons that are contained in this book

Contained in this book are many passages directly from FEMA publications. I did this to solidify the reasoning and thought processes that monitors must use every day. I also included the FEMA information, so you can refer to it while talking with a contractor.

Each deployment is different and must adhere to the Federal, State and Local regulations. This book is a general overview that will help you get a jump start on the rules and regulations. However, I have included notes pages at the end of each section, so you may note the special rules for the project you are working on.

I have made every attempt to include vital and accurate information. However, laws change, and administrative codes are revised. If you have questions about the accuracy of any single item, please review it with your supervisor.

Enjoy the book and enjoy your work as a debris monitor. Always remember, honesty, integrity and good work ethic are the three most important things a debris monitor must practice.

SAFETY IS ALWAYS FIRST

Legal Declaimer

The information contained in this book is for educational
purposes only. It is not intended to provide legal advice. All
parties involved in gathering information, writing and preparing
this book shall not be liable for any information contained within.
It is incumbent upon the reader to verify all rules and regulations
with their supervisor, we cannot guarantee that the rules as they
were at the time of publishing are the same as they are now.

As a Debris monitor, it is your responsibility to adhere to all
current laws and regulation pertaining to your job as a Debris
Monitor.

Contents

INTRODUCTION

As a monitor, you will be exposed to many safety hazards. In this chapter, we will review some of those hazards and how you should be prepared to handle them. Contained in this section is information gathered from experience as a Monitor, a Supervisor, and an Operations Manager. By no means is this a comprehensive list of every hazard, however, we hope to prepare you to handle any hazards that you may face. These are general rules for all monitors. In later chapters, we will add safety rules that are specific to each monitor's job.

Each morning when you report to work, your supervisor should hold a safety meeting for a few minutes. They will cover important safety topics. It is important that you pay attention and abide by the safety rules they cover. One of my favorite safety officers used to say, "You were alive and had two arms, two legs, and two eyes when you reported for work this morning and we want you to be the same when you go home tonight."

The most important thing you can use in any safety situation is common sense. Most situations you face are not dangerous if you are prepared and know what potential hazards are possible and how to handle them. As you read through this first part of the book, I hope to give you the tools to go home safe every night.

I will cover what Personal Protection Equipment (PPE) you should always have and wear. I will cover work practices that will help you stay away from hazardous situations and how to handle them as they arise. You will face everything from falling limbs to animal bites and many things in between. I would advise you to read this chapter several times and review it during your deployment to make sure you are practicing "best safety practices" and will stay safe and healthy.

While you are in the field, you must always be diligent about your personal safety. You must also be aware of potentially dangerous situations for the public. If you see a contractor engaging in dangerous or unsafe practices, you should let your field supervisor or safety officer know immediately. You cannot and should not give the contractor safety advice, but you should make sure that dangerous behavior is reported to your supervisors and they will handle the situation appropriately.

The company that hires you may also have a safety officer that should review many of these safety rules and recommendations. They will also be available to you to discuss any potential safety concerns you may have. Remember that Safety is the first chapter in this book because safety is your priority. It is hard to be a monitor from a hospital bed.

Always be safe and keep those around you safe.

PERSONAL PROTECTIVE EQUIPMENT

What is Personal Protective Equipment? According to OSHA,
*"Personal protective equipment, commonly referred to as "PPE",
is equipment worn to minimize exposure to hazards that cause
serious workplace injuries and illnesses. These injuries and
illnesses may result from contact with chemical, radiological,
physical, electrical, mechanical, or other workplace hazards.
Personal protective equipment may include items such as gloves,
safety glasses and shoes, earplugs or muffs, hard hats,
respirators, or coveralls, vests and full body suits."*

There are certain items that every monitor should always have
and wear while performing their duties. I will also make
recommendations of personal gear that may not be provided by
your employer. These items will make your job a little easier and
a little safer.

Hard Hat

The first piece of
PPE you need is a
hard hat. A hard
hat is a type of
helmet used by the
monitor to protect
their head from
injury by falling
objects, impact with other objects, debris, and other hazards.

Inside the helmet is a suspension system that spreads the helmet's weight over the top of the head so when the hard hat comes in contact with an object, the impact is less likely to be injurious to your skull.

I know many people think they have a hard head and they probably have been told that many times, but there is no substitute for a good hard hat. Your company will provide the appropriate hard hat. Do not go on eBay and buy one that has fancy designs and will make you look good. It may not be the correct hard hat for your job and may result in you being injured. So please, wear the hard hat you are given and look good after work.

Your hard hat should be worn when you are on the job site or get out of your car. Let me repeat that …. You **must** always wear your hard hat when you are outside your car or on the job site.

The reason you must do this is you never know where or when an accident may happen. So, when you are not protected by your car, you need to be protected by your hard hat. I got so used to wearing mine, I never took it off during the day.

Safety Vest

The safety vest is the next piece of PPE that you must always wear. I put mine on before I leave the house in the morning and never take it off until I returned home at night.

Your safety vest is not only important for your safety; it is a
requirement
under OSHA
rules. Any
worker that
will encounter
traffic is
required to
wear a high
visibility vest.
This vest is
usually either a
safety yellow
or safety

orange with reflective tape. This combination allows people to
see you at all times of the day.

There are many crazy drivers on the road and you need to have
your vest on and keep an eye out for those drivers that are
distracted and may not see you. In today's high-tech
environment, drivers have many things in their car that will
distract them. The next thing you know, they are slamming into
you. The vest helps them see you, but you must always be on the
lookout for people that do not pay attention. The vest is designed
to help them see you, but they must be looking. Wear your safety
vest, but also pay attention to those that may not be paying
attention.

Safety Glasses

The last piece of equipment that all monitors should have is safety glasses. These glasses are designed to protect your eyes from flying debris. Your hard hat protects your head from possible head injuries and your safety glasses protect your eyes.

It is hard to do this job if you are blinded by debris. You will be around chips from the cutting of limbs, dust from chipping,

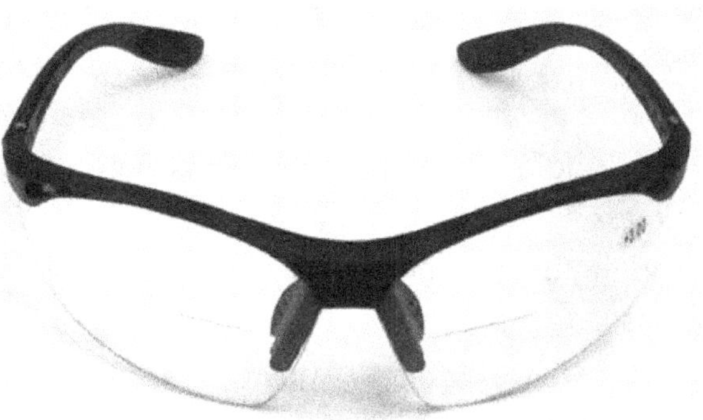

flying debris from loading of debris, etc. Always protect your eyes when you are outside your car.

Safety glasses are made from a high impact resistant plastic and usually come in either clear or with a tint for sun protection.

Your safety glasses should be worn at any time you are exposed to the possibility of flying debris or dust. Some people prefer to wear them like their hard hat, anytime they are outside of their car. I suggest you wear them, even if you do not feel there is a danger. Prepare for the unexpected and you will not be caught by surprise.

Dust Mask

Not all monitors will be issued a dusk mask as part of their standard PPE like their Hard Hat, Safety Glasses or Safety Vest. However, I think the dust mask is just as important. If you are a tower monitor and it is the middle of summer, the debris field will get awful dusty. No matter what your duty, if you encounter a lot of dust during working hours, you need to request dust masks from your supervisor.

Other

Other items you will wear every day are long pants and leather or protective boots. The long pants are required any time you are on the job site. You cannot wear shorts, capris pants, yoga pants or any other type of clothing that does not completely cover your legs. When on the job site you are exposed to many hazards, from poisonous plants to flying debris, that makes wearing long pants necessary. Most monitors like their pants to be a little heavier, like jeans, to protect their legs from flying debris.

Shoes are another item you need to consider carefully. Work boots that come above the ankle will give you ankle support when you are walking on uneven surfaces. Usually, these boots come with nonslip soles and many also have a steel toe. The steel toe boot comes in handy when someone decides to see what your toes will look like when a tree limb is dropped on them. You cannot wear heels, tennis shoes, slides or go barefoot. You must have proper footwear and proper foot protection. There are many types of work shoes. Make sure they are protective and comfortable, as your feet will be in them 12 to 14 hours a day.

Extra Equipment

There are some items that are not required, your company may not supply them but are handy to have in your car.

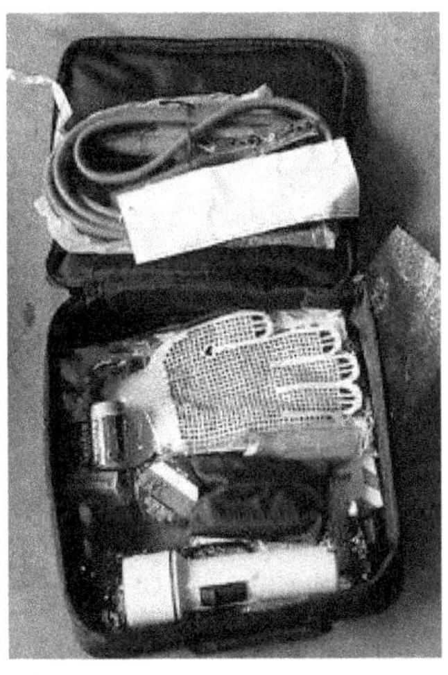

- Rain gear
- Changes of clothing appropriate for the location, weather, and assignment
- Alcohol-based hand sanitizer
- Flashlight with spare batteries
- Prescription medicine for the expected length of stay (with considerable safety margin)
- Over-the-counter medications for minor illnesses (e.g., pain reliever, allergy medication, hydrocortisone cream, antibiotic cream, bandages)
- Sunscreen (SPF-50 or higher. A dermatologist recommended I use baby sun protective lotion because it provides the best protection)

- Lip Salve
- Insect repellent
- Extra pair of glasses or contacts (If you wear contacts, anticipate dusty conditions at disaster sites)
- Jumper cables
- Tow chains

These items will make your job easier in the long run. Most can be picked up inexpensively at your local dollar store and will save you time and anguish while on the job. If any additional items are required, talk with your safety officer. They are there to make sure you go home every night with all the body parts you arrived with.

Summary

That sums up the "must haves" for all monitors. There are other safety items that monitors may need for specific jobs. If you are near water you may need a life vest, wader boots or snake chaps. In these cases, you need to get with your safety officer to find out what protective gear is appropriate for your situation. Your safety officer should be your best friend. Their job is to make sure that you go home each night safe and healthy.

ON SITE SAFETY RULES

There are many safety rules on the job site. It seems like every day; your safety officer will remind you of a new rule or tell you repeatedly a rule that some people just don't seem to follow. I will review some of these rules in this chapter. This is not an exhaustive list of all the rules, but they are some of the most important.

I ask you to read this chapter at least once a week. So many times, we go out in the field, day after day, and we start getting complacent. After working 80 hours a week for a few weeks, it seems like we know what the hazards are, so we think we are safe. It is when we get complacent that serious accidents occur. I know one monitor that was too busy talking on her phone and did not see the bucket swing her way. The next thing she knew, she was on the ground with a concussion from being hit in the head with the bucket. She should not have been inside the swing radius of the boom and she should not have been on her cell phone.

Read through these rules, pay attention to them, and read them at least once a week. Pay attention every minute you are on the job. It only takes a second of non-attention to get hurt.

Slips Trips and Falls

Slips, trips, and falls constitute most of the general industry accidents. They cause 15% of all accidental deaths and are second only to motor vehicles as a cause of fatalities. As a monitor, you will be working on many different types of surfaces and in many different environments.

We addressed proper footwear in the safety equipment section. Proper footwear plays a vital part in protecting you against a slip, trip or fall. I have witnessed people who thought clogs were proper footwear and they were out of work for 4 weeks with a sprained ankle. Keep your boots or protective footwear on while on the job.

<u>Watch where you step</u>. I have stood in many safety meetings listening to safety officers repeat, watch where you step, watch where you step and watch where you step…. You must always be aware of your surroundings and watching where you step. Sometimes, you have walked the same path a hundred times, but it only takes a second of non-attention to cause a slip, trip or fall.

When you are walking beside a road and there is tall grass, you never know when a hole is hidden under the grass.

When you are in that situation, try and walk on the road as much as possible. Walk where you can see where you are stepping.

You must also consider the surface you are walking on. If you are walking on a red clay road after a rain, it is going to be slippery. If you are walking along the side of a road that has deep grass, there may be hidden ruts and holes. If you are walking on an asphalt road after an ice storm, it is going to be slippery.

When you are walking among the debris, be extremely careful where you step. Loose debris and protruding debris can cause you to trip or fall if you are not very attentive to your surroundings. Use common sense and be attentive as you walk around the job site. It only takes a second of non-attention to cause an accident that may keep you out of work or worse.

If you can wear high top boots. These boots will help your ankle stability and may help prevent twisted or sprained ankles.

Your Car

You will be using your own vehicle. You need to obey all local traffic laws. That means obeying the speed limit and traffic control devices. You also need to make sure your seat belt is fastened whenever your car is moving. I have had many monitors complain that it was a pain to put on their seatbelt because they were in and out of their car so many times in a day. It does not matter if you are traveling 20 feet or twenty miles, your seat belt needs to be on. It is the law and likely a company safety policy, so buckle up for safety.

In the morning, before you report to work, you need to check your car to make sure you have gas to make it through the day. Check your fluids to make sure they are appropriate levels. Check your tires. Is the pressure correct? Are there any nails or slashes that could cause a flat tire? Make sure the car will carry you through the day, safely and hazard free.

Whenever I pass an auto parts store I like to go in and have them check my battery. When you are running your flashers most of the day you do not want to be stuck with a dead battery

When you park your car, park it in front of the contractor's vehicle. Many contractors will want you to park behind their vehicle. Their reasoning is so crazy drivers will run into your car first. For your safety, let them run into the contractor's vehicle first. You must park at least 100 feet away from the contractor's vehicle. You do not want to be in your car and see a limb drop, do a 2 and 1/2 somersault with a 1 and 1/2 twist and come right through your front window.

When you pull off the road to park, make sure the ground is hard and level. You do not want to park in driveways or block driveways. I had one monitor that insisted it was easier for him just to pull into people's driveways. He wasn't going to be there long, and he could move his car is people needed to get by. What he did not consider was his car leaked oil. The company got a call from the city manager and ended up having to have several driveways cleaned. Sometimes you may have to park 400 or 500 feet away to find a safe place to park. You do not want to call your supervisor to come and pull your car out of a ditch.

Whenever you park your car, turn on the emergency flashers. This may be a drain on your battery, however, it is essential to let drivers know that you are stopped, and part of the debris cleanup operation. Stop by a local Wal-Mart or automotive parts store and have your battery checked. If it is weak, it may leave you stranded after leaving your emergency flashers on for any length of time. If you exit your vehicle, do not leave it running. It may overheat or even worse, someone may hop in and go for a joy ride.

You turned off your car and have exited it. Before you leave the car, you need to lock it. Always make sure you have your keys with you before locking the doors. I went by Home Depot and picked up a magnetic key holder, so I would have an extra key just in case I locked my keys in the car.

Depending on which type of monitor you are, you may exit your vehicle 8 times a day or 60 times a day. No matter how many times you exit or return to your car, make sure you check for passing vehicles before entering or exiting your car. It is very important that you safely enter and exit your vehicle by checking for passing vehicles. Remember that you do not have to account for the time to exit the vehicle but also the time to walk around the vehicle to a safe position.

Do Not Use Your Cellphone whenever your vehicle is in motion. That means no texting, no talking, no surfing the web and no game playing on your phone. **Do Not Use Your Cellphone** when you should be paying attention to the debris operation. When you are on your phone, your attention is not on what you are doing. Some companies have made it a requirement

that their employees do not use their cell phones for anything but business during the workday. If your supervisor calls you during the day, do not answer until you are safely away from any debris operation and in a place, you feel is safe from possible hazards. You will be distracted while on the phone, so make sure you are away from any potentially hazardous situations. Remember, if you are in potentially dangerous situations, your cell phone becomes a distraction that may cause you a grave injury.

I was on a job site where a monitor was coming back to the job

site at the end of the day. He got a text about a party that night that he just could not wait to read. The next thing he knew he woke up in the hospital with no feeling from his neck down. To this day, he is still paralyzed and all because he could not wait to answer a text.

Remember, you are driving your vehicle. Keep both you and your vehicle away from potentially hazardous or dangerous situations. Keep your mind on the job and your cell phone use to a minimum and only when safe. ***DO NOT USE YOUR CELLPHONE!!***

Fatigue and Stress

You will be working 12 to 14 hours a day. The work is not strenuous, but the hours are long. If you find yourself in stressful situations on a regular basis, talk with your supervisor about the problem and what steps can be taken to reduce your stress level, as stress is a major contributor to fatigue. Many times, it is as simple as moving you to a different contractor.

If you are feeling very fatigued, again,

talk with your supervisor and explain to them what is happening.
If the fatigue is from partying after work, the solution will be
simple … quit partying and get some rest. No company wants an
employee that is extremely tired on the job because they tend to
make mental errors and become dangerous to themselves and
their fellow workers. Get plenty of rest and be alert. It only takes
one moment of inattention to cause serious injuries to yourself or
those working with you.

Heat Stress

Sometimes you will be working in conditions that are extremely
hot. Exposure to extreme heat can lead to illness and injury.
Heat stress can cause stroke, heat exhaustion, dehydration,
dizziness, cramps, and rashes.

The most common signs and
symptoms of heat stress include:

- Confusion
- Dark-colored urine (a sign
  of dehydration)
- Dizziness
- Fainting
- Fatiguc
- Headache
- Muscle or abdominal cramps
- Nausea, vomiting, or diarrhea
- Pale skin
- Profuse sweating
- Rapid heartbeat

During these periods of extreme heat exposure, there are some common rules you should follow.

- If you have air conditioning in your car, try and use it in down periods to lower your body temperature.
- Take rest/water breaks in areas that are shaded or air-conditioned when possible.
- Drink 4 to 8 ounces of water or sports drink every 15 minutes while working in hot, humid conditions.
- Limit fluids to no more than 1 ½ quarts per hour when working in hot, humid conditions. Do not drink more than a total of 12 quarts of fluid in 24 hours.
- Limit the intake of caffeinated and alcoholic beverages as they promote dehydration. Stay away from energy drinks, they are full of caffeine.
- Wear light-colored clothing and light cotton shirts.
- Know the signs and symptoms of heat stress. If you start exhibiting symptoms, let your supervisor know immediately.
- Consider the use of personal cooling devices.

Heat stress is very serious and should be considered whenever you are working in hot and humid environments. If you have any of these symptoms, sit down in a shady or air-conditioned space and drink some water. Do not drink ice cold water, drink water that is just a few degrees below the outside temperature.

Cold Stress

Cold stress is a very serious condition that occurs when the body can no longer maintain a normal temperature. The results can be serious cold-related illnesses and injuries, permanent tissue damage or death. A cold environment forces the body to work harder to maintain its temperature as it draws heat from the body. When working as many hours as monitors do, this can accelerate fatigue.

To help reduce the chance of cold stress:

- Wear layers of clothing that are windproof and waterproof. Consider keeping additional clothing with you and changing into dry clothing as soon as possible if work clothing becomes wet.
- Take rest breaks in warm, sheltered spaces or in your car.
- Drink plenty of fluids to prevent dehydration and limit the intake of caffeinated beverages.
- Know the signs and symptoms of cold stress (pain and numbness in the extremities, excessive fatigue, severe uncontrollable shivering, drowsiness, irritability) and report any of these to your supervisor.

Animal Bites, Stings and Aggressive Behavior

In some areas, you may experience exposure to insects and wild animals. You need to treat animals with respect. You are invading their home and they will try and protect it. Use proper insect repellent and proper insect sprays in areas that have insect problems.

If you encounter a large number of wild animals, let your safety officer know so they can get you proper PPE equipment,

- Use insect repellent containing DEET or Picaridin.
- Assume that all snakes are poisonous and that all animals are rabid.
- Be on guard for stray or wild animals, as they can exhibit unpredictable or aggressive behavior. If you see a wild animal or a snake, do not get out of your vehicle until it has cleared the area.
- Be cautious about where you place your hands and feet. Do not put your hands in holes or under objects (e.g., lumber, scrap metal, overturned boats) without checking to see if snakes, insects, or other animals are present.
- Deer ticks are carriers of Lyme disease. When working in high grass, cover exposed skin with long sleeves and pants as weather permits. Report all tick bites to medical personnel.

Sunburn

You will be working many days from sun up to sun down. During that time, you will be exposed to the sun a large period of the time.

- Wear sunscreen throughout the day. It is recommended to wear at least SPF-50. I personally prefer a sunscreen made for babies like Banana Boat Baby as it gives greater protection. You are not on the job to get a nice suntan, so protect your skin from overexposure.
- Whenever possible set up your work area in a shaded location
- Try and wear clothing and hats that will protect you from the sun.

Poisonous Plants

The most common problems with poisonous plants arise from contact with the sap oil of several ever-present native plants that cause an allergic skin reaction—poison ivy, poison oak, and

poison sumac.

If you encounter poisonous plants, you should:

- Immediately rinse skin with rubbing alcohol, specialized poison plant washes, degreasing soap (such as

dishwashing soap) or detergent, and lots of water. Rinse
frequently so that wash solutions do not dry on the skin.

- Scrub under nails with a brush.

- Apply wet compresses, calamine lotion, or hydrocortisone
  cream to the skin to reduce itching and blistering.

- Oatmeal baths may relieve itching.

- An antihistamine such as diphenhydramine (Benadryl) can
  be taken to help relieve itching.

Conflict Resolution

During your tenure as a
debris monitor, there may
be times when you and the
contractor disagree. You
must remember you are the
controller of the tickets and
a contractor cannot force
you to write a ticket. Here
are some tips to help you
resolve conflicts that you may encounter.

- Realize when the situation is beyond your authority or
  knowledge, and then contact your field supervisor for
  assistance.

- Respond … don't react. Don't let your emotions control
  the situation. Keep your emotions under control and you
  will be able to hear what others are trying to say and
  respond accordingly.

- Listen carefully without interrupting. The key here is LISTEN before speaking.

- Acknowledge the other person's position and then state how your position is different and why

- You need to give respect to get respect

- Communicate clearly and with proper respect so your viewpoint will be received with understanding and respect

- Identify points of agreement and disagreement

- Move the conversation away from justifying your position and toward resolutions

- Stick to the topic at hand and avoid inserting another disagreement

- Don't insert yourself into situations that are not within your authority or knowledge.

- Choose the proper time and place for the discussion

Remember, you are on the job to monitor the contractor and the contractor is on the job to complete the cleanup in a safe and timely manner. You need to work together so everyone can get their job done. If you, and the contractor you are assigned to, are constantly arguing, ask your supervisor to appoint you to another contractor.

UNDERSTANDING THE FEMA GUIDELINES

As a monitor, you must understand the FEMA guidelines and how they are interpreted in the field. One of the most important guidelines is very general but will be the basis for many decisions you must make.

Eligible debris work must be in the public interest, which is defined as work necessary to meet the following:

•   Eliminate immediate threats to life, public health and safety;
- *Eliminate immediate threats of significant damage to improved public or private property;*
- *Ensure economic recovery of the affected community to the benefit of the community-at-large*

The phrase *"Eliminate immediate threats to life, public health and safety'* is a very important phrase. You will run into circumstances that are not covered by a rule or regulation. In these circumstances, you must use this rule to help you decide. You are there to monitor the work being done and to make sure that the work complies with the FEMA guidelines and the guidelines of the government agency you are working for. You

are also there to make
sure that the immediate
threat to the public is
handled correctly and
removed. There are
also other rules
relating to eligible
debris.

*Eligible debris removal work under the Public
Assistance Program must meet the following criteria:*

- *The debris was generated by the major disaster event;*
- *The debris is located within a designated
  disaster area on an eligible applicant's
  improved property or rights-of-way; and*
- *The debris removal is the legal responsibility of the
  applicant.*

When they refer to the applicant, they refer to the city, county or
state that has hired you to monitor the cleanup. For example, if
you are hired by the county, your contractor cannot work on state
or city-owned property. You should be issued a map that clearly
marks the eligible roads and property that are maintained by the
government entity for which you are providing monitoring
service. If you have a question on whether a road or property
qualifies, be sure to ask your supervisor.

Those are the two main FEMA rules that govern all the other
specific rules that we will discuss later. What types of trees and
limbs are eligible to be cut; and what type of trees and limbs are
considered normal debris, and which are dangerous trees. They
are all separate rules but are governed by the two rules above.

Next, we will look at the
FEMA rules for the
individual monitor. What
their responsibilities are and
what they are expected to
do.

*The debris monitor's
roles and responsibilities in the field include:*

- *Validate hazardous trees, including hangers, leaners, and stumps (use appropriate documentation forms).*
- *Ensure that contractors are accurately credited for their load.*
- *Report to the project manager if improper equipment is mobilized and used.*
- *Report to the project manager if contractor personnel safety standards are not followed.*
- *Report to the project manager if public safety standards are not followed.*
- *Report to the project manager if completion schedules are not on target.*
- *Ensure that only debris specified in the scope of work is collected and identify work as potentially eligible or ineligible.*
- *Ensure that work stops immediately in an area where human remains, or potential archeological deposits are discovered.*
- *Report to the project manager if debris removal work does not comply with all local ordinances as well as State and Federal regulations.*
  The applicant is responsible for ensuring that applicant-managed debris removal work (either force

account or contract) being funded under the Public Assistance Program is eligible in accordance with Public Assistance Program criteria.

After you read all those duties, you must think that your responsibilities are quite expansive. It sounds like you are responsible for everything; however, it boils down to just a few simple rules. You watch, document and perform your job with integrity and you make sure that you and the public are never put in hazardous situations by the contractors.

It is your job to report, not to be the safety officer. It is your job to document, not tell the contractor how to do their job. It is your job, to be honest, and forthcoming in all your reports and documentation. It is that simple to follow FEMA's guidelines. Just remember to document all eligible work and let your supervisor know if the contractor is operating in a manner that puts you or the public at risk.

LEANER/HANGER MONITOR

A leaner/hanger monitor follows a contractor that is cutting dangerous trees and limbs. As a monitor, it is your job to determine if the tree or limb qualifies, under FEMA rules, and whether to issue a ticket for the contractor to be paid.

To accomplish that task, you must first know how to classify each one of the trees or limbs or stumps. This part of your job is very important because each one of the tickets you issue represents a payment to the contractor. You want to make sure you only give tickets for the trees that qualify, as these will be reviewed by your supervisors, the local government and FEMA.

The cutting you will be monitoring will be in one of three categories:

- Hazardous Trees
- Hazardous Limb Removal
- Hazardous Stumps

In the next several pages, we will review each one of these classifications and how to determine if they qualify. These pages need to be read several times and understood completely. If you have any questions about any of the classifications, be sure to ask your supervisor to review it with you.

Remember, each ticket you produce is a pay document and represents a payment to the contractor. It is very important to make sure that the work qualifies under FEMA guidelines or rules given you by the local government agency you are working for.

Hazardous Trees

Determining a tree as hazardous is one of the jobs of the monitor. A monitor cannot tell the contractor which trees to cut, or how to cut them, but they can say whether they will issue a ticket for the tree. A ticket is what the contractor gets paid by, so if you are not going to give them a ticket for the tree, most likely, they will not cut it.

Removing a hazardous tree may be eligible for FEMA reimbursement, so you want to make sure that the tree qualifies under FEMA guidelines.

" A tree is considered hazardous if its condition was caused by the disaster; it is an immediate threat to lives, public health and safety, or improved property; it has a diameter breast height of six inches or greater; and one or more of the following criteria are met:

•   It has more than 50 percent of the crown damaged or destroyed;

- It has a split trunk or broken branches that expose the heartwood;

- It has fallen or been uprooted within a public-use area; and/or
- It is leaning at an angle greater than 30 degrees"

So, the first three questions you must answer are:

1. Was damage caused by the disaster?
2. Is it an immediate threat to lives, public health and safety, or improved property?
3. Is it greater than 6" diameter at breast height?

Then you need to determine whether the tree qualifies by one of the four additional criteria. Unlike the first three, the tree only must qualify by one of the additional criteria. So, let's review what all that means one statement of the time.

It has more than 50 percent of the crown damaged or destroyed

First, let's look at the definition of the crown of a tree. The tree crown is the top part of the tree, which features branches that grow out from the main trunk and support the various leaves.

While all trees feature a crown, several types of crowns adorn different types of trees. For instance, a pine tree has a very long trunk and small crown and an oak tree has a shorter trunk and larger crown.

Now comes the common-sense part. The tree may have 50% of its crown destroyed by the storm, but if it is not an immediate threat to lives, public health and safety, or improved property, does it qualify? According to FEMA, it should be cut, however, they have disqualified these sometimes because they did not pose an immediate danger. They have said if the tree is not leaning, has a lot of damaged branches hanging or in some way qualifies as an immediate threat, then it does not get cut. If it does, it gets cut as close to the ground as possible. However, check with your supervisor to see how the local government wants this type of situation handled.

Many contractors will want to cut every tree as a dangerous tree, but it must qualify as an immediate threat. If you have a question about a tree or your contractor refuses your determination, call your supervisor to get a second opinion. Many times, you can take a picture of the tree and send it to your supervisor's phone instead of having them come out to the site to look at the tree themselves.

If there is a dispute between you and the contractor, make sure you describe your position completely to help your supervisor understand your call before talking with the contractor.

You are the monitor and you control the tickets, so make sure your decision is correct. You do not want to limit the contractor's ability to do their work, however, you also want to make sure that the work they do qualifies for payment.

It has a split trunk or broken branches that expose the heartwood

If a tree has the heartwood of the trunk exposed, it is going to die very quickly. There are some experts that contend they can fix trees that are split and expose the heartwood, but you are in a cleanup project that has limited time to remove potential dangers to the public. FEMA has determined that it is more cost effective and time efficient to remove this type of tree. This type of tree should be cut at ground level or as close as possible.

It has fallen or been uprooted within a public-use area

Remember that the tree needs to be at least 6 inches in diameter at breast height. Again, there are some interesting determinations you must make. One, the contractor can only remove that part of the tree that extends into the public area. If the trunk of the tree is on private property and the branches are in the right of way; the

contractor can only cut those branches that extend into the right of way.

If the tree is less than 6 inches in diameter, it is considered regular debris and should be removed by the debris collection trucks. There is also another exception. When the trunk is broken at less than 5 feet from the ground and the tree is lying on the ground it is considered regular debris and not a dangerous tree. Again, we run into ambiguous determinations. FEMA says in their rules that if it is fallen or uprooted, it qualifies as a dangerous tree and must be cut, however, if the tree is lying on the ground it is considered regular debris. This is again a situation where you need to discuss with your supervisor how the local government wants to handle this situation.

Trees determined to be hazardous and that have less than 50 percent of the root-ball exposed should be cut flush at the ground level. The cut portion of the tree is included with regular vegetative debris. The contractor should try to cut the tree trunk as close to the ground as possible.

The eligible scope of work for a hazardous tree may include removing the leaning portion and cutting the stump at ground level.

The tree is leaning at an angle greater than 30 degrees

This type of tree is called a leaner. Many companies will only let supervisors qualify a leaner. However, if you know what a leaner is you can quickly identify if a tree is a leaner. Is the tree leaning at 30 degrees or more? This means that the tree is leaning 30 degrees or more from 90 degrees vertical.

When I was in the field I used an app on my smartphone that was a level. I held it up as I was looking at the tree and if it was below 60 degrees, it was a leaner.

There are trees that grow at an angle. The easiest way to determine if the tree has been growing at an angle is to look at the limbs. If the limbs have started growing at 90 degrees from the ground, then the tree has been growing at an angle and was not damaged by the storm. Also look at the root ball. Is the root ball coming loose from the ground? If so, then the tree was probably damaged by the storm.

Lastly, remember that a leaning tree must be an immediate threat to lives, public health and safety, or improved property and at least 6 inches in diameter.

Hazardous Limb Removal (Hangers)

Hanging limbs are the next category of tree dangers that must be cleared and qualify for FEMA funding. Just like dangerous trees, hangers must meet strict criteria to be eligible for FEMA reimbursement. You, as a monitor, must document the cutting of hangers that qualify. Limbs must be:

- Located on improved public property;
- Greater than two inches in diameter at the point of breakage; and
- Still hanging in a tree and threatening a public-use area, e.g. trails, sidewalks, right of way

The first thing to remember about the cutting of hanging limbs is the contractor gets only one ticket per tree no matter how many hanging limbs are in the tree. They must also remove all hangers that are in the tree. If the tree that the contractor has had cuts on it before, you cannot give them a ticket. That is why it is important for them to remove all hangers the first time.

While a tree may have 5 hangers in it, only one of the hangers must qualify.

If the canopy of a tree located on private property extends over a public right-of-way such as a sidewalk, removal of hazardous limbs on the tree that extends over the public right-of-way and meet the above criteria may be eligible. Limbs on the tree that do not extend over the public right-of-way are not eligible.

In my experience, hanging tree limbs are the most discussed and argued over the type of cut. The contractor will try and get as many trees as he can to qualify with hangers and the monitor must be diligent and only qualify those that are truly a danger to the public.

I have had contractors tell me that a limb, 20 feet outside the right of way was going to fall, bounce a couple of times, do a somersault, and end up in the middle of the road. COMMON SENSE. You as a monitor must use common sense.

If the hanger is on the back side of the tree and it falls, is it going to hit a car going down the road? If you are in a heavily wooded area and there are trees between the road and the limb, is there a chance, when it falls, that it will hurt anything except a beetle in the woods.

Remember the third criteria, is it a danger to the public if it falls.

Lastly, you may not cut a limb that will fall on private property. You are only clearing dangers that are a danger to the public. The individual homeowner is responsible for clearing any dangers on their own property.

Hazardous Tree Stumps

A stump may be determined to be hazardous and eligible for stump removal if it meets all the following criteria:

- It has 50 percent or more of the root-ball exposed (less than 50 percent of the root-ball exposed should be flush cut);
- It is greater than 24 inches in diameter, as measured 24 inches above the ground;

- It is on improved public property or a public right-of-way; and
- It poses an immediate threat to life, and public health and safety.

If an uprooted stump must be removed prior to FEMA's approval, the following information must be submitted.

- Photographs and GPS coordinates that establish the location on public property;
- Specifics of the threat;
- Diameter of the stump 24 inches from the ground; and
- Quantity of material needed to fill the resultant hole.

Unlike dangerous trees and hanging limbs, hazardous tree stumps need prior approval from FEMA before they are removed. You should document the location of the stump, the threat, and the size so the contractor can submit that information to FEMA for their approval.

Do not issue a ticket for a hazardous stump unless FEMA has given their approval or you supervisor has determined that the stump is an immediate danger and must be removed immediately. If a stump is less than 24 inches, then the stump is treated as regular debris and is picked up by debris trucks.

Most monitors will never issue a hazardous stump ticket.

Safety and Miscellaneous Rules

For a Leaner/Hanger Monitor, there are additional safety rules and there are a few rules that only apply to them.

The first rule is; when the contractor is cutting the tree; do not stand in the drop zone. This means you should be at least 100 feet away from the tree being cut. I say, at least, because if you are cutting a 120-foot tree, you should be about 200 feet away.

In a recent deployment, a monitor was standing by the contractor's truck and a big limb was cut. When it fell, the monitor thought he was going to be hit so he ran out of the way. He ran into traffic, was hit and killed.

In another instance, a monitor was standing too close and a limb dropped on his foot and broke almost every bone in his foot.

Yes, standing 100 feet away means you are going to have to walk a little more, but at least you will be walking. Remember to use common sense and keep yourself out of the drop zone.

While we are on safety, let's talk about your shoes. Of all the monitoring jobs, the Leaner/Hanger monitor is probably the one that needs steel toe boots the most. I would strongly recommend that you wear leather steel toe boots.

Next, let's discuss some of the special rules for Leaner/Hanger monitors. You are responsible for measuring the trees and limbs to make sure that they meet FEMA qualifications. The broken limb must be at least 2 inches and the tree must be at least 6 inches. When measuring the tree, make sure you measure the true diameter of the limb or tree.

I have seen contractors take a 1.5-inch limb and cut it at a diagonal and convince the monitor to measure the long way to qualify the limb at 2 inches. Remember the section on fraud. That is fraudulent and is purposely providing false information to the government to pay that contractor.

When measuring the tree or tree limb, wait until all cutting on that tree is done. If a tree has 4 hanging limbs, do not run up to measure the first one cut. Wait until they are all on the ground.

When you are ready to measure the limb, the contractor's groundsman will pick up the limb they want qualified for you to measure. You do not touch the limb. You do not crawl through the brush to get to the limb. Let the groundsman choose the limb and bring it to a safe place for you to measure.

Now let's talk about what we call keeping at arm's length. You will be working closely with the contractor for weeks. You will get to know each other. While being friendly is fine, remember you are there to monitor the job they are doing, and you do not want anyone to think your integrity has been compromised. Here are a few rules to follow to make sure there is no appearance of impropriety:

- Do not ride in the contractor's vehicle and do not let any contractor employee ride in your vehicle.
- Do not accept money, food, drinks or anything of value from a contractor.
- Do not go out with or visit a contractor employee outside of work.

Keep your relationship professional. If a contractor offers you money or anything of value for additional tickets or qualifying trees that should not be qualified, report it immediately to your supervisor.

You may be a very honest person and would never participate in a fraud, but just the appearance of impropriety may cost you your job or worse. Be diligent and professional at all times.

Tree Identification

This tree limb fell, and part of the limb was in the right of way. You can see that the contractor trimmed the branches at the

property line. When you are wondering where the property line is, a good indicator is a fence, utility line, water meter, etc. This tree was trimmed at the fence line.

This tree has a broken limb, but it is not in the right of way. However, this tree is in a public park and is a very real danger to the public.

This tree has a tree limb that is broken but is not attached to the tree. While the limb can probably be pulled down, it is still a hanger. The contractor may have to cut several limbs to get it out of the tree. These types of hangers are very dangerous and pose a real danger to the public.

This tree is broken at the beginning of the crown. That means if you just cut the broken part of the tree, you would leave a very large stump that has no chance of living. In this case, the

contractor would cut it as a dangerous tree and cut it as close to the ground as possible.

This is another example of a detached hanger. If these hangers are close enough to the ground, sometimes the debris trucks will latch on to them and pull them down. As you can imagine, the danger from this type of hanger increases every time the wind blows.

This picture shows two dangerous trees. The first one closest to the camera is a leaner and the second one has the crown completely broken off. The problem with these trees is there is no way to only cut them off at the property line. To remove these trees, the contractor would have to get a "right of entry" signed by the homeowner. This would be done because the trees originate in the right of way and there is no way to remove the danger by cutting the tree at the property line.

This tree would not qualify for a ticket. Since the trunk below the break is less than 5 feet, the tree would be considered regular debris and the debris truck crew would collect it and cut the stump at ground level. Also, you may notice that the tree has fallen into the woods so no ticket for the ROW crew either.

This tree is considered a dangerous tree. It is a leaner. It poses an immediate danger to the public, it is in the right of way and is leaning at greater than 30 degrees. The tree would be cut at ground level and the debris truck would  pick up both the tree debris and the stump.

RIGHT OF WAY MONITOR

The right of way monitor (ROW) has the task of monitoring the trucks that clean up the debris from the storm. This debris may fit into many categories such as vegetative, household goods, hazardous, and several others.

Let's start out with a few safety reminders for the ROW monitor.

- When you get out of your car make sure there are no cars approaching. You could lose your door, or we could lose you.
- When you stop, always stop at least 100 feet in front of the truck you are monitoring.
- When you stop, put on your emergency flashers to signal drivers you are part of the debris clean up team.
- Try and walk on the road and away from tall grass as much as possible
- While the truck is loading, you must stay at least 100 feet away from the loader
- When you give the driver the load ticket, do so from the passenger door. Do not go out into traffic to deliver a load ticket.
- Pay attention and be aware of dangerous drivers. See them because they are usually not paying attention, so they don't see you.
- Wear you Hard Hat and safety vest whenever you exit your car.

These are just a few of the safety rules we mention earlier. Read them every day and practice them every day. Your safety is a top priority.

Your truck that you are following will be picking up one type of debris. They cannot pick up vegetative and hazardous debris at the same time.

Because there are several categories of debris, the monitor must always watch the truckload to make sure they are only picking up qualified debris and they are picking it up from the public right of way.

The ROW debris monitor's roles and responsibilities in the field include:
- Complete and physically control all load tickets (in monitoring towers and the field).
- Ensure that trucks are not artificially loaded to maximize reimbursement (e.g., debris is wetted, debris is fluffed - not compacted).
- Ensure that hazardous waste is not mixed in with loads.
- Ensure that all debris is removed from trucks at the DMS.
- Report to your supervisor if improper equipment is mobilized and used.
- Report to your supervisor if contractor personnel safety standards are not followed and pose a threat to you and the public
- Report to your supervisor if public safety standards are not followed.
- Ensure that only debris specified in the scope of work is collected and identify work as potentially eligible or ineligible.

- Ensure that work stops immediately in an area where human remains, or potential archeological deposits are discovered.
- Report any damage to public or private property caused by the contractor and fill out an incident report on each incident.
- Always monitor the contractor to ensure that only eligible debris and proper debris is being picked up.
- Make sure that the contractor is not picking up from private property or undeveloped property.

Let's review some of these rules and why they are important. *Keeping physical control of the load tickets.* This is very important because each one of those tickets represents money to be paid to the contractor and the potential for fraud is great if the contractor can handle the tickets prior to you properly filling them out.

If you have an electronic device, you always keep that on your person. I have had monitors leave the electronics in the contractor's truck, on the bumper of the contractor's truck and one just misplaced it. That device represents money being paid. It is like an ATM machine. Once a ticket is printed the contractor gets money. You must treat it like it was your own personal credit card and protect it from abuse.

Make sure that trucks are not artificially loaded. There are many ways for a contractor to scam the system. I have seen contractors try many ways to get a few extra dollars on each load. When the loads are weighed they can wet the load or put water in the bed to increase weight. When measured by volume, they can try and stack the debris so there are a lot of air gaps and try and cover it so as not to be recognized. There are as many ways to scam the system as there are roads in the state. It is your responsibility to remain alert and report any suspicious activity to your field supervisor. As you can see from the example truck here, they fluffed the branches instead of compacting the load. While the contractor was looking for a high load percentage, his true call would be very low.

Ensure debris is removed at the DMS. Again, some contractors are looking for a little edge and will not completely remove all debris at the dump site. This means that they are getting paid twice for the debris. Make sure every time your contractor starts, they start with an empty truck. On a debris site, I did not work, a truck would come in with a full load and take the load out the other side of the site full because the monitoring company did not have a monitor in a tower on the exit. The truck would leave the site then return an hour later and repeat the same thing.

Another way they try and cheat on the loads is they will go out at night and load debris that does not qualify and then get the monitor to give them a ticket for the load first thing in the morning. That is why a monitor must verify that the truck is empty in the morning before it starts loading and empty each time it comes back from the dump.

Ensure only proper debris is loaded. This one is where a lot of contractors tend to try and cheat. You will be monitoring for a specific government entity. Let's use a city as an example. If you are monitoring for a city, you may only remove debris from city right of way. You cannot touch debris on a county or state road. You may not remove debris from private property. You cannot go out in the woods to find old dead trees. You cannot pull up live vegetation. These are just a few things I have witnessed. For that reason, it is important that you always pay attention and diligently watch the contractor perform their duties.

Report safety hazards and violations. For both your safety and the safety of the public, you must report to your field supervisor any safety violations that you witness. While it is not your job to be a safety officer for the contractor, it is your job to make sure that proper safety procedures are being followed so the public is not put in danger.

Load Ticket

Traditionally, load tickets have been carbon paper tickets with at least four copies generated for one load of debris. More advanced tracking tools have been developed and used in the field to reduce human error and expedite funding. These computer-based

The term "load ticket" refers to the

Load Ticket Information	Monitor Ticket	
	Load Site Collection	DMS or Landfill
Preprinted ticket number	NOT APPLICABLE	
Contract number	Contractors may be Identified by number	
Prime contractor's name		
Date	X	
Truck number	X	
Truck driver's name	X	
Vegetation	X	
Construction & Demolition	X	
White Goods	X	
Household Hazardous Waste	X	
Other (required to be described	X	
Load Location	GPS or	
Loading date/time (departure from collection location)	X	
Loading Site Monitor name/signature	X	
Truck capacity in cubic yards or tons		X
Load Size, cubic yards or weight (percent of actual)		X
Unloading location		X
Unloading date/time (arrival at disposal		X
Unloading site monitor name/signature		X

systems often include the same information as a traditional load ticket. Each monitor is responsible for filling out specific areas of the load ticket. The table lists the load ticket information and the portions of the ticket to be completed by the respective monitor.

Each monitor keeps a copy of the load ticket, and the driver/contractor keeps two copies for billing purposes.

In computer-based systems, the collection monitor gathers the same information as in a traditional paper load ticket system and inputs this information into a handheld digital device. The ROW monitor gives the hauler the information in a digital or paper format. The Tower monitor, stationed at the DMS or landfill, gathers the information and completes the transaction in a manner like the traditional method. The Tower monitor can then print a ticket for the hauler's billing purposes. These tickets are very important because they contain all the information needed for the hauler to get paid and for the government entity to verify what they are paying for. Each type of debris will have a different code and different pay scales, so it is important to be correct in the load type and the amount of debris.

Equipment

The most typical unit measurement for vegetative and construction and demolition debris is the cubic yard. Debris trucks are measured and tagged at the main site. Once they are measured and the capacity is determined, the truck is tagged with an identification number, so the ROW and Tower monitors can easily identify the truck and its capacity.

Most contractors must use appropriate equipment to load debris efficiently so that the maximum level of compaction can be achieved to facilitate removal of debris from the public right-of-way. For

example, a truck that is loaded by a skid steer cannot be compacted as well as a truck with a loading boom. However, on smaller roads and in small neighborhoods, the larger trucks may have a problem with clearance. In these situations, a skid steer may have to be used and their loads would be discounted appropriately at the DMS site.

Types of Debris

Vegetative Debris

Vegetative debris consists of whole trees, tree stumps, tree branches, tree trunks, and other leafy material. Depending on the size of the debris, the collection of vegetative debris may require the use of flatbed trucks, dump trucks, and grapple loaders.

Most vegetative debris consists of large piles of tree limbs and branches that are piled on the public rights-of-way by the residents. The collection

of this type of debris is eligible for reimbursement if it is within public rights-of-way and collected by an eligible contractor.

Normally the government entity will limit the number of times the debris is collected; for instance, the applicant may choose to make two passes throughout the jurisdiction before resuming its normal collection activities. This is done so that the residents can remove debris from their property that was generated by the storm. The first pass usually is the largest pass.

The contractor may also have a person who cuts trees that do not fall under other FEMA guidelines. Examples of this are trees that are less than 6 inches in diameter but pose a threat to public safety. This may also include trees that are lying on the ground or are broke at less than 5 feet from the ground.

Construction and Demolition Debris

The definition of construction and demolition debris may vary between States. Construction and demolition debris can be defined as damaged components of buildings and structures such as lumber and wood, gypsum wallboard, glass, metal, roofing material, tile, carpeting and floor coverings, window coverings, pipe, concrete, fully cured asphalt, equipment, furnishings, and fixtures. To be eligible, construction and demolition debris must be a result of a Federally declared disaster.

Certain types of construction and demolition debris are reusable or recyclable; while others may be classified as hazardous material. Each government entity will handle this type of debris differently. You will be trained, and guidelines will be given to you for the handling of this

type of debris as outlined by the government entity you are
monitoring for.

Typically, removal of construction by-products generated
by repairs or rebuilding is covered by insurance policies or
included in the overall cost for reconstruction projects;
therefore, it is not eligible debris. You must make sure that
the construction debris being picked up is from damaged
structures, not new construction.

Hazardous Waste

Hazardous waste is waste with properties that make it
potentially harmful to human health or the environment.
Hazardous waste has at least one of the following four
characteristics: ignitability, corrosivity, reactivity, or toxicity.

Certified hazardous waste
technicians should handle,
capture, recycle, reuse,
and dispose of hazardous
waste. At no time should
the regular trucks that
pick up other types of

debris pick up hazardous waste. These pick-ups will be
done by special contractors and will be disposed of in a
proper manner.

Household Hazardous Waste (HHW) refers to hazardous
products and materials that are used and disposed of by
residential, rather than commercial or industrial consumers.
HHW includes some paints, stains, varnishes, solvents,
pesticides, and other products or materials containing volatile
chemicals that catch fire, react, or explode under certain
circumstances, or that are corrosive or toxic.

Electronic waste, or e-waste, refers to electronics that contain hazardous materials such as
cathode ray tubes. Examples include computer monitors and televisions.

Unlike vegetative debris that gets one ticket when the truck is loaded, hazardous waste gets a ticket for each item that the contractor picks up. That means one ticket for each TV, each solvent, etc.

White Goods

White goods are defined as discarded household appliances such as refrigerators, freezers, air conditioners, heat pumps, ovens, ranges, washing machines, clothes dryers, and water
Heaters

Soil, Mud, and Sand

Floods, landslides, and storm surges often deposit soil, mud, and sand on improved public property and public rights-of-way. Facilities commonly impacted by this type of debris may include streets, sidewalks, storm, and sanitary sewers, water treatment facilities, drainage canals and basins, parks, and swimming pools.

The contractor will remove the soil, mud or sand and the monitor will produce tickets for the work as instructed by their field supervisor. Since not all removal is covered under FEMA Guidelines, you will need to get specific instructions as to what is and is not covered.

Vehicles and Vessels

To remove and dispose of a vehicle, the following criteria must be met.

- The vehicle or vessel presents a hazard or immediate threat that blocks ingress/egress in a public-use area;
- The vehicle or vessel is abandoned, e.g. the vehicle or vessel is not on the owner's property and ownership is undetermined;
- The government followed local ordinances and State law by securing ownership; and
- The government verified chain of custody, transport, and disposal of the vehicle or vessel.

As a monitor, you must make sure that each step is followed and documented.

Putrescent Debris

Putrescent debris is any debris that will decompose or rot, such as animal carcasses and other fleshy organic matter. The gathering and disposal of this type of debris is done by a special contractor and should not be mixed with regular debris.

Infectious Waste

Infectious waste is waste capable of causing infections in humans, including contaminated animal waste, human blood and blood products, isolation waste, pathological waste, and discarded sharps (needles, scalpels, or broken medical instruments).

Most instances, this type of waste is collected and disposed of by a federal agency. Again, this type of waste should not be gathered and disposed of with other types of waste.

Chemical, Biological, Radiological, and Nuclear-Contaminated Debris

Chemical, Biological, Radiological, and Nuclear (CBRN)-contaminated debris is debris contaminated by chemical, biological, radiological, or nuclear materials because of a natural or man-made disaster, such as a Weapon of Mass Destruction (WMD) event. Eligibility determinations on the clearance, removal, and disposal of CBRN-contaminated debris will be made by FEMA based on applicable Federal statutes, regulations, policies, and other guidance documents. Depending on the nature of the disaster and the debris it generates, FEMA may develop additional or disaster-specific eligibility guidance.

If you encounter waste that falls into this category, immediately remove yourself from the area and contact your field supervisor.

Garbage

Garbage is waste that is regularly picked up by the government by its normal contractors. Common examples of garbage are food, packaging, plastics, and papers. In general, household food wastes can be collected through normal municipal waste collection methods and are not part of storm debris collection.

TOWER MONITOR

The tower monitor is one of the most important monitors, as they complete the document cycle started by the ROW monitors in the field. The trucks fill up with debris in the field and then come to the DMS site to dump what they have collected.

There are two types of measuring the truckload. One is by weighing the load and the other is by determining the amount of the debris in the truck or trailer. The first, weighing the truck is straightforward. The truck comes in full and the truck leaves empty. The difference of the weight coming in and going out is what determines what the contractor is paid for that load.

The second type is by volume. How much debris is in the truck in cubic yards. This is the more difficult because the monitor must determine what percentage of the truck is loaded. This is not how high it is stacked or how much of the truck is showing, it is the actual cubic yards.

Since this is the more difficult, we will spend more time explaining how this is done and how to estimate the volume as accurately as possible. An example is a bunch of oak tree limbs that have not been compacted. There are a lot of air gaps in the load and FEMA does not pay contractors to haul air.

Guidelines

• Check the truck number on the placard.
• Check that the capacity (size) of the truck written on the ticket matches the size marked on the side of the truck.
• Walk around the truck. Make sure that the truck is loaded with disaster debris. Ensure that the truck is not falsely loaded.
• When the truck leaves, make sure it is completely empty.

• If there is no tailgate on a truck, the truck is not full. The maximum estimate of the capacity of the load is 85 percent full. However, the monitor must use good judgment to determine if the load is really 85 percent. It is more likely that the truck is between 40 percent and 60 percent full.
• There are other percentage variations of how a truck can be loaded
• A truck is 100 percent full only when the debris is filled completely to the brim and the truck is heaped above the sideboards. The truck must have a tailgate that secures the entire back end of the truck. It is very rare that a contractor can achieve a 100% full. It is difficult,

though not impossible, for a truck to be 100 percent
loaded because woody debris, trees, branches, and rubble
cannot be placed in a truck without having air holes. The
other reason it is almost impossible to get 100 percent is
local laws usually prohibit debris being piled above the
sideboards or hanging out the side.

Determining A Load

When you are determining the cubic yards in a load, you will
usually determine the percentage of debris that is filling the truck.
This is usually done in 5% increments, like 95%, 90% and so on.

This truck is loaded to the top and the debris has been compacted. This load could be called at 95%. Very few trucks will ever be loaded 100% unless they are hauling water or sand. You must also make sure the trucks are not piled so high as to present a safety hazard. You will be in a tower above the truck, look, and lean over and make sure there are no gaps in the truck bed that are empty.

This truck has come to the dump site with far less than a full load. We cannot see into the truck from this picture, but it appears the load is a maximum of 60% and then when we can look inside we would reduce that amount from the gaps and quality of compacting.

Equipment limitations impact the maximum loading capacity of some vehicles. The following is a list of truck conditions and the eligible capacities.

Hand-loaded trucks and trailers cannot achieve compaction levels comparable to mechanically- loaded vehicles. This effectively reduces the capacity of the hand-loaded truck or trailer in comparison to a truck or trailer that is loaded mechanically. Therefore, FEMA only reimburses 50 percent of the debris monitor's observed capacity percentage for a hand-loaded truck or trailer.

Example: If a hand-loaded truck or trailer appears to be 80 percent full and would normally be recorded at 80 percent, that load should be recorded at 40 percent. You must also consider if the truck is loaded with a skid steer type loader that cannot reach into the bed and compact the load. If this is the case, you must consider it like a hand loaded truck.

As you can see from this picture, there is no compaction of the branches which leaves a lot of gaps and a lot of airspace.

A truck with no tailgate or no solid tailgate cannot be compacted to its full capacity; therefore, FEMA only considers a maximum of 85 percent of the certified truck capacity for payment to the contractor

Truck without a tailgate. Its maximum load capacity is reduced to 85 percent. This truck is claimed to be 'fully loaded' with branches sticking above the top and beyond the back of the truck bed—the actual load is only 75 percent. Also, a truck loaded like this poses a hazard to the public.

These two pictures are directly related to each other. The first is the picture of the truck as it came into the dump site. It is a 20 cubic yard container and was determined to be 85% full. The contractor would have been paid for 17 cubic yards.

The load was then dumped (the picture on the right) and measured. The measurement showed that it was 4 cubic yards. That mistake, made over thousands of truckloads, would cost hundreds of thousands of dollars.

This trailer does not have a tailgate, so it starts at 85%. Then the trailer is only about 80% full and is not well compacted so this load would be 60%. This is an example of what contractors may try and get away with.

This trailer has a bunch of tree tips that are not compacted at all. This is like a hand loaded trailer and so it is about 50% full and take 50% of that and you get 25%. If you give the contractors a score like that, which they deserve, they will load the trucks and compact their loads better before bringing them to the dump site.

Tower Monitoring Tips

Monitors should be aware of situations that could impact FEMA's payment for the debris collected.   They should be on the lookout for:

Inaccurate Truck Capacities - Trucks should be measured before operations and load capacities should be documented by truck number. Periodically, trucks should be pulled out of operation and re-measured by the applicant.

Trucks Not Fully Loaded - Do not accept the contention that loads are higher in the middle and if leveled would fill the truck. Monitors may check to see if that statement is valid. The monitor has the last word in the determination of how full the truck has been loaded.

Trucks Lightly Loaded - Trucks arrive loaded with treetops (or a treetop) with extensive voids in the load. Trucks need to be loaded to their full capacity with front end loaders or other similar equipment. A truck that is loaded with tree tops will not get a high percentage because of the air gaps. You are judging how full the truck is if it was compacted.

Trucks Overloaded - Trucks cannot receive credit for more than the measured capacity of the truck or trailer bed even if the material is above the sideboards. If a truck is measured to carry 18 cubic yards, it cannot receive credit for more than 18 cubic yards. However, it can receive credit for less if not fully loaded or lightly loaded.

Changing Truck Numbers - Normally, trucks are listed by an assigned vehicle number and capacity. There have been occasions where truck or trailer numbers with a smaller carrying capacity have been changed to one with a larger capacity. For instance, a 20-cubic-yard truck may have a number for a truck that can carry 30 cubic yards. This can be detected if the applicant periodically re-measures the trucks or records actual State license plate numbers in addition to a description of the truck.

Reduced Truck Capacity or Increased Truck Weight - There have been occasions where trucks have had heavy steel grating welded two to three feet above the bed after being measured, thus reducing the capacity or inflating the weight of a load. This can be detected by periodically re-measuring the truck bed or recertifying the truck tare weight. You must also look at the bed of the empty truck every time the truck leaves the site. This will allow you to make sure it is completely empty and there are no cheater bars in the truck.

Wet Debris When Paid by Weight - Excessive water added to debris will increase the weight of the load. When the contractual unit cost is based on weight, this increases the amount paid the contractor. Contractors have added excessive water to debris loads to increase the weight when being paid by the ton. This can be detected during monitoring if there is excessive water dripping from the truck bed or by inspecting the truck bed immediately after unloading. The applicant should periodically recertify the truck tare weight.

Multiple Counting of the Same Load - Trucks have been reported driving through the disposal site without unloading, then re-entering with the same load. This can be detected by the monitor inspecting the truck before it leaves the DMS and ensuring the truck is empty.

DOCUMENTATION

As a monitor, your job is to monitor the activities of the contractor and document those activities for payment. There are several different ways that this documentation is accomplished.

<table>
<tr><td colspan="2">JACKSON COUNTY SOLID WASTE</td><td colspan="2">LOAD TICKET
#</td></tr>
<tr><td colspan="2">Applicant:</td><td colspan="2">Disaster #</td></tr>
<tr><td colspan="2">Program:</td><td colspan="2">Contractor:</td></tr>
<tr><td colspan="2">Truck # :</td><td colspan="2">Truck Capacity:</td></tr>
<tr><td>House # :</td><td colspan="2">Street Name:</td><td>Zone #:</td></tr>
</table>

Debris Classification:

- ☐ Vegetative/Woody
- ☐ Mixed
- ☐ Construction & Demolition
- ☐ White Goods
- ☐ Household Hazardous Waste
- ☐ Animal Carcasses
- ☐ Hazardous Materials / Toxic
- ☐ Other:____________

<table>
<tr><td>Driver's Name:</td><td>Loading Odometer:</td></tr>
<tr><td>Loading Time:</td><td>Loading Date:</td></tr>
<tr><td colspan="2">Monitor Signature: I.D. #</td></tr>
</table>

= =

<table>
<tr><td colspan="2">TDSRS / Disposal Site Location:</td></tr>
<tr><td>Load Call (%):</td><td>Disposal Odometer:</td></tr>
<tr><td>Disposal Time:</td><td>Disposal Date:</td></tr>
<tr><td colspan="2">Monitor Signature: I.D. #</td></tr>
<tr><td colspan="2">Contractor Signature: I.D. #</td></tr>
<tr><td colspan="2">Notes:</td></tr>
</table>

White - Applicant   Yellow and Blue - Contractor   Pink and Green - Driver   Gold - Site Copy

Work Tickets

The first way is the old fashion pen and paper. On that sheet the monitor will include:

- Date and time
- Location of the hazard that was removed; either the GPS location, street address or similar information;
- The hazard removed, either hazardous trees, limbs, or stumps;
- Name of the debris removal contractor that performed the work;
- name of the debris monitor that provided oversight for the work and
- Pictures of the hazard before and after the removal
- Measurement of the hazardous tree, limb or stump

These were 4-part forms and the monitors had a GPS and camera to use to document the work.

Many companies now are switching to an automated system that use smartphones or tablets in the field that speed up the collection of information and step the monitor through the process, so all information needed is collected and properly documented.

Since each company has their own system, whether old fashion or automated, it would be impossible to review their operation in this book. What we can do is go step by step through the documentation process, so you know each step and understand why that information is needed.

The date and time of each action is needed. This is for verification of when the action was taken. It is impossible for a contractor to cut 10 qualifying trees in 10 minutes or to cut 400 trees in one day. Your supervisors will look at the type and number of tickets being generated to make sure that the work being performed is possible.

The location of the tree, limb or stump is needed for verification purposes. Your supervisor, the local government, and FEMA will spot check the locations and review the work done to make sure the work is eligible under FEMA guidelines.

The type of hazard removed is needed to pay the contractor the proper amount. Each type of hazard and size of that hazard may have different pay scales.

The contractor's name is needed so all the tickets for that contractor can be grouped for payment.

The monitor's name is needed, so if there are any discrepancies, or problems with the ticket, the monitor can explain and correct the problems.

Pictures of the hazard are needed to make sure the hazard qualifies under FEMA guidelines and that the work being paid for was completed. This picture is important in the verification process. When you take the picture do not take it of the trunk or straight up the tree like the pictures here. Neither picture would qualify the tree as a hazard.

The picture of the tree needs to be of the tree and show the proximity to the right of way. So, in your picture, you need to take it from a distance that will allow you to get both the tree and the right of way in the picture. This picture shows the tree as a hazard and would be used to justify the cutting of the tree.

Make sure your pictures are of both the tree and the right of way. It is very important.

The measurements of the hazard are needed to make sure that the hazard qualifies and that the contractor is being paid properly based on the size of the hazard.

Those are the basic information needed for the contractor to get paid. Remember that each ticket you generate is like writing a check from FEMA to that contractor. Make sure all the information is included and you are only issuing tickets for FEMA qualified work.

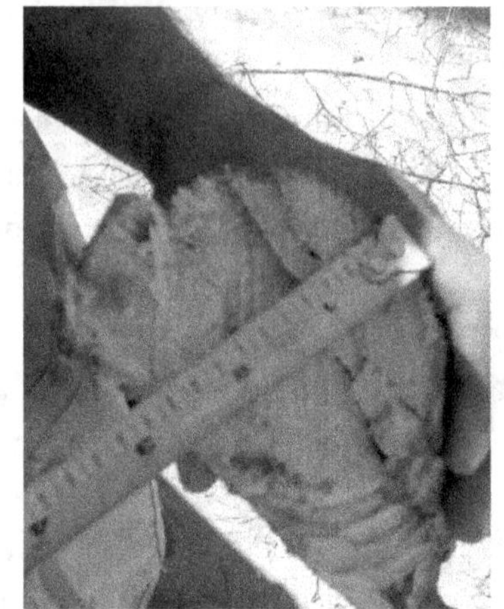

Daily Logs

There are several types of daily logs that are used in the field. Each company has their own set and they differ from company to company.

The first type of daily log is the monitor's log. If you are using the old fashion paper and pencil type of system, the log keeps track of the information on the tickets. This log will contain the summarized information from each ticket, so your supervisor or company has a very concise way of looking at your work.

The second type of log is a daily issue log. This log is used by the monitor to report any issues you may encounter in the field. Examples may be the contractor cut a limb and it fell and broke a homeowner's fence, or the contractor was backing up and hit a car. These issues must be documented on the log with pictures. If it is a safety issue, you will want to document it and contact your safety officer, so they can get a more detailed statement as to what happened.

As a leaner/hanger monitor, these are the main types of logs you will be faced with. Other types of monitors and supervisors will have different logs that they will fill out.

Fraud

The maximum penalty for conspiracy to defraud the United States is five years in prison and a $250,000 fine. Generating a fraudulent work ticket for a contractor is a very serious crime. It is committing fraud against the federal government.

There have several cases brought against individuals based on the issuance of fraudulent work tickets. One such case involved $750,000 in fraudulent tickets and 4 people ended up in jail, they were ordered to pay restitution and they were given over $500,000 in fines.

You, as a monitor, are there to make sure that the work being performed qualifies for payment and that the work is performed. If you make an error in judgment as to whether a tree qualifies or not, it is not a crime, however, if you give tickets for work that is not performed, that is fraud.

Terms

Applicant –State agency, local government, or eligible private nonprofit organization that intends to apply for Federal Emergency Management Agency (FEMA) Public Assistance (PA)Program grants.

Construction and Demolition Debris–FEMA Publication 325 defines construction and demolition (C&D) debris as damaged components of buildings and structures such as lumber and wood; gypsum wallboard; glass ;metal; roofing material; tile; carpeting and floor coverings; window coverings; plastic pipe; concrete; fully cured asphalt; heating, ventilation, and air conditioning systems and their components; light fixtures; small consumer appliances; equipment; furnishings; and fixtures. Current eligibility criteria include the following:
- Debris must be located within a designated disaster area and be removed from an eligible applicant's improved property or right-of-way (ROW).
- Debris removal must be the legal responsibility of the applicant.
- Debris must be a result of a major disaster.

Debris - Items and materials broken, destroyed, or displaced by a natural or man-made federally declared disaster. Examples of debris include, but are not limited to, trees, construction and demolition material, and personal property.

Debris Clearance - Clearing roads by pushing debris to the roadside to accommodate emergency traffic.

Debris Management Site (DMS) - A location where debris is sorted, processed, reduced in volume, and/or disposed of (debris management activities at a permanent disposal site).

Debris Monitoring - Actions taken by applicants to document eligible quantities and reasonable expenses during debris activities to ensure that the work complies with the contract scope-of-work and/or is eligible for Public Assistance grant reimbursement.

Debris Removal - Picking up debris and taking it to a debris management site, composting facility, recycling facility, permanent landfill, or other reuse or end-use facility.

Debris Removal Contractor–The debris removal contractor is contracted to remove and dispose of debris that is a result of a severe debris-generating event.

Hanger–A hanger is a hazardous limb that poses a significant threat to the public. The current eligibility requirements for leaning trees according to FEMA Publication 325 are as follows:
- The limb is greater than two inches in diameter.
- The limb is still hanging in a tree and threatening a public use area.
- The limb is located on improved public property.

Hazardous Stump –A stump is defined as hazardous and eligible for reimbursement if all the following criteria are met:
- The stump has 50 percent or more of the root ball exposed.
- The stump is greater than 24 inches in diameter when measured 24 inches from the ground.
- The stump is located on a public ROW.
- The stump poses an immediate threat to public health and safety.

Hold Harmless - Generally, a contractual arrangement whereby one party agrees to hold the other party without responsibility for damage or other liability incurred by an action or transaction.

Household Hazardous Waste–The Resource Conservation and Recovery Act defines hazardous wastes as materials that are ignitable, reactive, toxic, or corrosive. Examples of household hazardous waste (HHW) include items such as paints, cleaners, pesticides, etc. Due to the nature of hazardous waste, certified technicians must be used to handle, capture, recycle, reuse, and dispose of hazardous waste. The eligibility criteria for HHW are as follows:

- HHW must be located within a designated disaster area and be removed from an eligible applicant's improved property or ROW.
- HHW removal must be the legal responsibility of the applicant.
- HHW must be a result of a major disaster.

Leaner–A tree is considered hazardous and defined as a "leaner" when its present state is caused by a disaster, the tree poses a significant threat to the public, and the tree is six inches in diameter or greater when measured at chest height.
The current eligibility requirements for leaning trees according to FEMA Publication 325 are as follows:

- The tree has more than 50 percent of the crown damaged or destroyed (requires written documentation from an arborist).
- The tree has a split trunk or broken branches that expose the heartwood.
- The tree has fallen or been uprooted within a public use area.
- The tree is leaning at an angle greater than 30 degrees.

Legal Responsibility - In the context of debris management, a statute, formally adopted legal code, or ordinance that gives local government officials responsibility to perform work on public and/or private property.

Monitoring Firm –The monitoring firm is an organization under contract with the local government to monitor debris removal operations. The monitoring firm ensures the debris removal contractor is working within the scope of work contracted by the local government and documents debris removal operations.

Right of Entry - As used by FEMA, the document by which a property owner confers to an eligible applicant or its contractor or the United States Army Corps of Engineers the right to enter onto private property for a specific purpose without committing trespass.

Right-of-Way - The portions of land over which facilities such as highways, railroads, or power lines are built. It includes land on both sides of the facility up to the private property line.

Vegetative Debris–As outlined in FEMA Publication 325, vegetative debris consists of whole trees, tree stumps, tree branches, tree trunks, and other leafy material. Vegetative debris will largely consist of mounds of tree limbs and branches piled along the public ROW by residents and volunteers. Current eligibility criteria include the following:
- Debris must be located within a designated disaster area and be removed from an eligible applicant's improved property or ROW.
- Debris removal must be the legal responsibility of the applicant.
- Debris must be a result of a major disaster.

White Goods–As outlined in FEMA Publication 325, white goods are defined as discarded household appliances such as refrigerators, freezers, air conditioners. The eligibility criteria for white goods are as follows:
- White goods must be located within a designated disaster area and be removed from an eligible applicant's ROW.
- White goods removal must be the legal responsibility of the applicant.
- White goods must be a result of a major disaster